POSITIVE PSYCHOLOGY:

Research and Applications of the Science of Happiness and Fulfillment

NEW FIELD, NEW INSIGHTS

JONNY BELL

D1534076

WHY YOU SHOULD READ THIS BOOK

This book will help you understand a revolutionary branch of psychology: positive psychology. Positive psychology, jolting from the traditional, depressing psychologies of day's past, prescribes the ways in which you can find true, internal satisfaction. It no longer lingers upon what is wrong with you; instead, it pushes you to ask: what is right with me and how can I improve upon that? How can I utilize my talents in order to maximize my life while I'm living it and achieve true self-satisfaction. You can be happy in the face of adversity and stress. You can push beyond lack of confidence, pessimism, and helplessness in order to achieve your goals and reach self-actualization? The book outlines research-driven concepts to allow true happiness to implant itself in your life. It quantifies decades of understanding about what makes humans happy or unhappy, and lands with a firm grasp on: yourself.

TABLE OF CONTENTS

Chapter 1. Comprehending Positive Psychology

Positive Psychology: the new psychology revolution swooping through the world, is asking the most interesting question: how can one be happy? Positive Psychology is the inverse of what is traditionally termed "regular" psychology. While regular psychology works to rectify psychological problems, to instill hearty, better mental states after mental trauma, positive psychology works to build positivity and satisfaction in normal life. The swerve from mental instability psychology to positive psychology is relatively recent; the interest in health and mental growth churned to the scene sometime in the past half century after many years of pegging people into mental institutions and studying their brains. Why not study the brain of a health person and try to scientifically administer greater health and happiness upon that person's life? Why not work to discover the ways in which a person can work toward a better, more fulfilling life? These are the general questions behind the exciting new field.

Positive Versus the Negative

Essentially, the "regular" psychology school's focus upon faltering human development doesn't tell the entire story of a person's brain life. Simply knowing what occurs in the brain after stress, after schizophrenia has kicked in, or after emotional trauma has occurred lends the view of a ruptured brain. One can completely understand how a "ruptured brain" works—or ultimately falters on a cellular, minute level. But how can one understand the ruptured brain without paying attention to a full, hearty brain? The full, hearty brain begins with all of its "pieces" in place: that is, it's healthy, full of vibrancy. Nothing is going wrong. However, most brains start out in this normal state. Something: life experience, choice, or environment triggers the brain to ultimately falter or reach to great, happy heights. The topic of positive psychology, then, tries to study the happy, healthy brain in order to help other brains to reach this magnificent, positive balance. Just as traditional psychology works to rectify a faltering brain, positive psychology works to push the brain forward: to ultimate life and joy.

THE OVER-ARCHING GOAL OF POSITIVE PSYCHOLOGY

The ultimate goal of positive psychology on a personal-level is, essentially, to learn the ways in which one can think through the neuron path to joyful emotions. Negative thoughts—on a drastic level—lead to brain disorders and counter-intuitive living. Therefore, positive psychology provides the idea that positive thoughts lead to brain growth and fulfillment. Of course, these positive thoughts—brought on a very person-level—vary from person to person. Not all emotions are the same.

Furthermore, "positive emotions" are not meant to completely eliminate negative emotions. Human beings have immense subtlety; basic positive emotions are swayed and "colored in" by gray, negative emotions.

Think of an example: a person achieves great success and graduates from a university. One would think that this person feels the utmost satisfaction at the graduation ceremony: after all, he's worked through many achievements and had to think positively for many years in order to reach this goal. However, for very personal, environmental reasons, his graduation ceremony may be "colored in" by a negative emotion. For example, his father could have died the previous year, therefore missing out on his graduation and lending him feelings of sadness. This does not work against the feeling of joy he feels for graduating; instead, this negative emotion fills out the satisfactory feeling, giving it a complete, human edge. Despite the unhappiness he feels, he still feels immense joy. It's complicated: but what involving humans isn't complex?

THE THREE ISSUES OF POSITIVE PSYCHOLOGY

Positive psychology looks to three main issues during its research and analysis of the human brain and body.

POSITIVE EMOTIONS

Positive emotions study the ways in which a person is happy and content with one's past events, happy in one's present situation, and hopeful for one's future. Therefore, one can feel pleasure from these three sectors. One can remember things that happened in the past and feel joy; alternately, past events can haunt a person, causing unfortunate mental blockings on the road to happiness. One can feel happiness from the hope one feels for the future. This can range from big ideas to small ideas. One can be happy about Christmas around the corner or fueled with the passion to study law in the coming years at a major university. Either of these situations brings hopeful joy. Present joy varies from day to day, obviously, based on current environmental factors. Positive psychology studies the ways in which one's present environment works against or fuels a happy mindset. It studies the ways in which the present brings satisfaction.

POSITIVE INDIVIDUAL TRAITS

Positive individual trait studies in the field of positive psychology lend an understanding of the ways in which a person's talents bring satisfaction and life joy. These talents could be natural: the ability to sing or dance, for example. They could be fueled by one's work environment: the talents one brings to the office in order to write the next big news story or work through the goals of the company. Everyone has inner strengths, inner virtues to push them toward a better, more fulfilling life. Not everyone uses these strengths and virtues wisely. Many are wasted.

POSITIVE INSTITUTIONS

The positive institution methods are based upon the strengths and virtues that stem from various institutions in one's life. These institution-led strengths bring joy and fulfillment to a community of people—providing a unit of safety and inclusion throughout a group. This, essentially, brings a level of relationship joy and satisfaction. It provides something to reflect one's self upon: one can compare one's self to the satisfaction of the community. If the community is fulfilled, provided with institutions that lend fulfilling relationships, one can assimilate into this environment and prosper.

Chapter 2. History of Positive Psychology

Understand the intricate history of positive psychology and the great waves it has created in the past fifteen years.

The Early and Mid Twentieth Century

Prior to the Second World War, psychology worked much like it does today: it worked to cure all mental diseases via mental hospitals and therapists; it worked to provide fulfilling and satisfactory lives for patients; and it worked to identify high talent and further that talent's way into the greater world.

Unfortunately, the years after World War II changed everything. Psychology became primarily cure-based. Therefore, there wasn't a sense to improve something that wasn't already broken. This could have been a result of the war; the nation had been through great traumas, and improving that which had been broken was on the minds of everyone. Abnormal behavior and mental illnesses had to be squashed. Post-traumatic stress disorder (PTSD) hadn't been recognized yet; however, psychologists knew the tragedy of war on the human brain in a very broad sense. They worked to repair it.

Abraham Maslow

During these subsequent "abnormality-focused" years after World War II, a few psychologists chose to focus on humanistic psychology. Abraham Maslow was one of these driving forces, one of the first in the game.

While working alongside Gestalt psychologist Max Wertheimer and Ruth Benedict, an anthropologist at Brooklyn College, Maslow was incredibly alert. He found both Benedict and Wertheimer to be exceptional: highly attuned to themselves, to their happiness, and to their careers. He later took note of their sure happiness and success as he cultivated his humanistic psychology.

Abraham Maslow created theories about self-actualization, peak experiences, and hierarchy of needs.

The hierarchy of needs displays five stages that a man must attain in order to focus on his internal happiness. One must first maintain one's biological health; afterwards, one can find safety, a place to call one's home, relationships, self-esteem fulfillment, and—ultimately—self-actualization.

SELF-ACTUALIZATION: MASLOW'S THEORY

Self-Actualization, one of Maslow's humanistic psychology theories, prescribes the idea that what a man can become, he must become. If he has met the other four stages of the hierarchy of needs and sees his potential laid out before him, he must reach that potential. It is the idea that one can become more full, more complete in one's self.

Self-actualization affects people in incredible ways, according to Maslow's theory. Self-actualized people take joy in solving problems in the greater, external world: problems that don't involve them. They feel a sense of personal responsibility. It allows for a deep sense of appreciation; self-actualized people see the world around them with a sharp eye, every-understanding that their lives are incredible, that each experience brings a sense of wonder.

Furthermore, self-actualized people reap the rewards of solitude. They enjoy their human relationships, of course; after all, relationships lie on the third step of the hierarchy of needs. However, the self-actualized person needs a few hours to breathe by himself every single day. This way, he can focus on who he wants to be and meeting their full potential.

The self-actualized person further reaches another one of Maslow's theories. He reaches peak experiences. The peak experience is a moment of ecstasy: one cannot fully grasp the intense joy one fells during these experiences. It is a moment of pure bliss. Afterwards, one feels completely rejuvenated and electrified. These peak experiences actually inspire one to further one's life, to reach for greater self-actualization.

Abraham Maslow's work is incredibly important; he pushed the limits of psychology from the 1950's mainstream, abnormal-focused realms. His theories are currently widely accepted with the resurgence of positive psychology.

MARTIN SELIGMAN AND THE RESURGENCE OF POSITIVE PSYCHOLOGY

1998 brought the election of the new president of the American Psychological Association. Martin Seligman stepped up to the position, bringing with him a new psychology theme: positive psychology. He lent all the modern ideas currently utilized and researched today: that the mind can ultimately decide to be joyous and satisfied and happy. In 2009, just eleven years later, the first World Congress on Positive Psychology took the reigns in Philadelphia, allowing the world to understand the research and the explosion of life-affirming science currently pulsing from the realms of positive psychology. At the convention, Seligman was a featured speaker. These days, he is widely regarded as the ultimate father of positive psychology.

Chapter 3. Positive Psychology Research Analysis

The scientific drive to discover the environmental, physical, and emotional factors that create a life of worth provides much room for exploration. All-inclusive psychology brings a humongous research field: one that closely analyzes the ways in which people live and eat and sleep and interact. It seems bizarre that something as subtle and throw-away as a smile could actually bring a world of scientists together in a room to discuss the science of happiness; however, positive psychology is a broad, subtle field. Scientists are opening doors into the window of the brain to discover just what creates satisfaction; they are looking to allow the greater, future populations to snatch that happiness through scientific understanding.

As aforementioned, there are three broad, over-arching themes of positive psychology: positive thinking, positive characteristics, and positive institutions. These three issues create three subplots in which scientists delve into the positive psychology of the mind. Look to the following research analysis in order to understand the very real findings, the very real scientific research scientists have discovered in order to create this mega-field.

Research in Happiness and Positive Thinking

SMILES: A BASEBALL-DRIVEN RESEARCH ANALYSIS OF THE POWER OF SMILE ON ONE'S LONGEVITY

How does one readily research a smile and determine whether or not it produces a happy, hearty life?

Researchers in positive psychology, Abel and Kruger, studied 150 baseball cards from 1952 to find out. In those days, there wasn't the ready "game face" associated with being a sport's player; therefore, the players generally produced a natural look for the camera, one that represented a true personality.

Abel and Kruger made a list of the players who had a Duchenne smile, players who had a subtle Duchenne smile, and players who did not smile at all. Note: a Duchenne smile utilizes all the face muscles around the mouth, lending a brilliant, natural smile. Think of Julia Roberts: classic Duchenne. Everyone has a Duchenne smile; not everyone uses it.

Their findings? 42% of the players were not smiling, 43% of the players were smiling a little bit, and just 15% of the players were demonstrating the full, outright Duchenne smile. What does this mean? One photo can't quantify one's entire life, right?

However, after calculating their Duchenne smile amounts: no smile, a little smile, or a big, natural smile, Abel and Kruger looked at the players' ages of death. The results were staggering. Players who did not smile in the baseball card photo had an average death-age of 72 years old. Players who smiled just a little bit had an average death of 75 years old. Players with the full Duchenne smile? They lived, on average, to a full 80 years old.

Incredible. Looking at this research alone, a Duchenne smile tacks a good eight years onto an average lifespan. It's important to note that the smile does not itself cause a longer life; rather, the smile is meant to reflect the interior, positive emotions of the person pictured. If one is happy, yielding a positive thought-cycle and a positive life, one's smile in the baseball picture might reflect that, lending insight to the following fifty years of joy and subsequent death at approximately age 80.

WHO SAVORS THE LITTLE THINGS IN LIFE?: A RESEARCH-DRIVEN ATTACK ON THE POWER OF MONEY

Positive psychology researchers Jordi Quoidbach, Elizabeth W. Dunn, K.V. Petrides, and Moira Mikolajczak investigated the question: which class group generally savors the small things in life? Where is the link between money and happiness, really?

These researchers created a study in Belgium in order to understand the link between income and little, life pleasures. They asked these people to fill out a survey lending insight into their daily lives; they wrote their income information, their natural disposition or lack thereof to enjoy the little, small pleasures in life, and what they thought was their lives' overall happiness.

While they filled out the study, half of the participants saw a photo of euros, reminding them of the power of money overarching in their lives. The other half was not reminded of these euros.

The findings of this study saw that the people who were reminded of lurking money by the photo of the euros on the wall reported lower abilities to savor the small things in life. Furthermore, the research found that the higher the people's incomes were, the lower their pleasure for little things was.

The positive psychology researchers took this a step further in Canada. They conducted the same study but then also asked people to munch on a chocolate bar. This chocolate bar is meant to sit in for "a bit of life-savoring." Therefore, the participants were timed as they were eating the chocolate bar, lending insight to how long they enjoyed the tiny life pleasure. Participants who enjoyed the chocolate bar longer were thought to have enjoyed it more rather than those participants who scarfed it down.

During this study, half of the participants were also shown a picture of money. The people who ate chocolate while being exposed to the money photo actually munched on their chocolate far quicker than the other participants, lending the link that money reduces one's pleasure in the little things. Furthermore, participants with a higher income actually seemed less likely to enjoy their chocolate bar.

FAST FOOD: AN IMPATIENCE-DRIVEN RESEARCH ANALYSIS OF HAPPINESS AND IMPATIENCE

Fast food has another downfall beyond its obvious health deterrents: it actually reduces one's happiness, making one far more impatient than normal. This seems counter-intuitive; after all, fast food is termed "fast" for a reason, right?

Naturally, researchers analyzed the behavior of college students in order to undertake this impatience study. While completing another task on a computer, the participants were "flashed" a number of fast food symbols: symbols from KFC, Subway, Burger King, Taco Bell, McDonald's, and Wendy's. Afterwards, the participants were asked to read from a short passage. There was no time limit; it probably seemed like a strange request. However, participants who had been flashed fast food logos, on average, read much faster than the other participants, therefore showing their impatience.

Another study asked participants to recall the events of the last time they either journeyed to a fast food restaurant or went grocery shopping. Afterwards, the participants completed an un-related marketing survey, one that didn't call attention to either grocery shopping or fast food. Participants who had been asked to recall their most recent trip to a fast food restaurant were much more likely to gravitate toward those marketing products on the survey that helped them save time. They demonstrated their desire to get things done quickly; they demonstrated their inherent impatience.

The fast food impatience findings are generally ironic. The inclusion of fast food in one's life leads to general dissatisfaction with the rest of one's life. Therefore, one is saving time by utilizing the fast food services in order to rush off and be impatient some place else.

POSITIVE CHARACTER STRENGTHS: THE RESEARCH

Remember that character strengths are the skills and intrinsic, personalized values in a person. These researchers attempted to categorize and quantify the research of generalized skill.

SOCIAL CLASS AND SKILL LEVEL

Positive psychologists, when studying human positivity, must take into account a remarkable characteristic: social class. One might not think one's social class makes a difference on one's level of positivity; however, research shows that social class alters thoughts, feelings, and actions dramatically.

Positive psychologists Michael Kraus, Stephanie Cote, and Dacher Keltner conducted an experiment to study social class and skill level; social class was formulated, in this experiment, as an independent variable. Through their research, they discovered that lower class individuals operated much better on an emotional, skilled level than individuals from the upper class.

The positive psychologists discovered that lower class individuals have a greater empathic understanding; therefore, they can infer other people's emotions and feelings. Empathic understanding is a humongous skill, one that results in greater maneuvering of the world. The study argued, of course, that lower class individuals have less control over their lives; therefore, they have been able to hone their empathic understanding in order to maneuver and read the people around them, in order to truly prosper in their community.

SAINTS VERSUS SINNERS: A RESEARCH-DRIVE ANALYSIS TO DISCOVER HUMAN GOODNESS

Goodness can be described as a skill; one's inherent decisions and abilities to treat the surrounding world with kindness can set one apart incredibly from one's peers.

However, when analyzing the "type" of person someone is: whether that person is an inherently good or bad person, it's important to understand this basic component of positive psychology: one is never inherently good or bad. One simply has degrees of both. Therefore, there is a great scale along which everyone aligns. This scale demonstrates personality; it does not differentiate between "type" of people because different types of people do not exist.

Therefore, can one describe people as happy people or unhappy people without looking at the range each person holds his happiness or sadness?

Researchers McGrath, Rashid, Park, and Peterson analyzed the surrounding world to discover if there were "evil" people and "good" people, if they could find the dividing line, the remarkable "character" line that sets these people apart. They couldn't. There are people, generally, who contain higher degrees of "good." Therefore, they are more likely able to be good. There are people who contain higher degrees of "bad." Therefore, everyone has it in them to be very good or very bad. Everyone can reach toward the higher dimensions of being "good," even if one currently resides on the lower side of being "bad." This is good news for the human populations: that one can alter one's degrees of positive characteristics and work toward greater positivity via the understandings of positive psychology.

POSITIVE CHARACTERISTICS OF HABITAT: DOES IT MATTER WHERE ONE RESIDES?

A resent positive psychologist study analyzed the positive psychology of various residences across the United States. This is converse to the traditional psychology research of cities; generally, cities are portrayed negatively, analyzing the negatives: the mental instability, the affinity for obesity, etc. This research was meant to understand the positive characteristics found in each city.

The study worked to prescribe arenas of love of learning, teamwork, and kindness via a survey. It was found that the strength of these positive arenas varied in relation to the city features: it related to how the city fared economically and subsequently voted in the later 2008 election. Note: the research was conducted between 2002 and 2005.

Compare two cities: San Francisco and Omaha, Nebraska. The people of San Francisco had greater head positive characteristics; therefore, they were more inclined toward intellectual and cultural properties. They voted for Barack Obama in the election: the liberal candidate.

Omaha, Nebraska, on the other hand, was found to have more heart-related positive characteristics. They imbibed less innovation and voted for John McCain in the 2008 election. The Omaha residents reported a greater sense for the meaning of life, leading one to believe that heart-positive cities were generally happier while head-positive cities were constantly searching for something greater.

POSITIVE INFRASTRUCTURE AND RELATIONSHIPS: THE RESEARCH

How does one study one's community and discover the positive psychology integrated in the walls of relationships, of the greater world?

THE INFANT STUDY: INFANT-DRIVEN RESEARCH ABOUT THE PERCEPTION OF INFANTS

What is going on in a baby's brain? Are babies simply a blank slate, or is there a bit of knowledge lurking behind those eyes? This research attempted to understand that which is lurking—the ways in which babies perceive the greater infrastructure around them. Everyone begins this way: as a baby, therefore, it is important to understand where one has come from and where one can go. One can be an infant and one can become a sociopath; however, where does it all begin?

Recent Yale-driven research showed that infants prefer good guys. This doesn't seem so bizarre; after all, the good guys usually give them something to eat and something to drink. Not so bad. However, the Yale study lends a real insight.

The babies were held up to watch a puppet show. During the puppet show, one puppet helped another puppet up a large incline to find a bouncing ball. Another puppet, all the while, tried to inhibit these actions. After the puppet show, the infants were asked to choose which puppet they wanted to touch or pick up. 80% of the time, the infants chose the good puppet, therefore indicating that some sort of preference for niceness occurs prior to language.

GRATITUDE-DRIVEN RESEARCH: A LITTLE THANKFULNESS GOES A LONG WAY

Allowing people to understand one's thankfulness creates a complete, gratitude-driven infrastructure. Other research has led the understanding that gratitude creates an emotional, relationship bond between people. It is central in human development.

Jeffrey Froh, Giacomo Bono, and Robert Emmons created a study to analyze the gratitude element in the group of people so often associated with lack of gratitude: the youth. Children from approximately 10 to 17 seem to lack the ability to yield their gratefulness, sometimes, lending frustration to their parents and peers.

The survey on 700 middle school students asked them to analyze a time when they were incredibly grateful. Afterwards, they measured their social integration in their current school and their life satisfaction. Students with greater gratitude showed greater life satisfaction via their enhanced social integration. Their gratitude had bound them to relationships, rendering them a boost of life-affirming interaction.

HAPPILY EVER AFTER: RESEARCH ON LIVING OUT THE REMAINDER OF LIFE

A 25-year study investigated the happiness of German people from 1984 to 2008. Every year, the German people involved in the study lent insight to their life happiness and fulfillment.

19

Via this study, researchers have understood one very important thing: happiness is not totally pre-determined by genes.

This pre-determination of happiness has been long-spouted. This is referred to as the set-point theory: that everyone is born with a determined happiness level that can temporarily boost or decline based on life events. Headey and his colleagues, in their German research, discovered that biology does not factor into happiness as much as psychological factors, rendering the belief that one can alter one's happiness.

Generally speaking, the Germans who reported the greatest life fulfillment and happiness reported having an emotionally stable life partner; they prioritized their family's life goals; they attended church regularly; they balanced both their leisure life and their working life, rendering a complete understanding that both are important for fulfillment.

CHAPTER 4. ACHIEVING HAPPINESS

Happiness is at the forefront of positive psychology. It is the seed from which all other positive psychology grows.

According to Martin Seligman, the father of modern positive psychology, happiness contains three different roads. All of them are necessary roads in order to meet the great backbone of positive psychology: happiness and joy for one's surroundings and life.

1. Gratification and Pleasure. These are very basic, every day feelings, feelings associated with human functions like eating and sleeping and watching a movie. One feels pleasure and then feels instant gratification and joy.

2. Maintaining Strengths and Virtues. Therefore, one understands one's skills and strengths and utilizes them, thus walking down the path to self-fulfillment.

3. Life purpose. This line of happiness involves one's strengths and virtues assigning to something important, something greater than one's self. It allows one to co-exist in a greater community and feel that one is necessary, that one's life is not meaningless.

THINKING CONSTRUCTIVELY FOR TRUE HAPPINESS IN PAST, PRESENT, AND FUTURE TENSES

In order to feel truly happy, one must think constructive thoughts about one's past and feel true optimism for one's future.

It is an oft-thought phenomenon that one should deal with the past with angry feelings; that one should express those angry feelings in order to "expel" them. However, Seligman notes that East Asian techniques that force quiet mental states actually allow one to cope with stress and work toward the road to happiness. If one expresses negative emotions, they live on for a greater amount of time.

Looking toward the future, Seligman reports greater happiness in those with high amounts of optimism and hope.

The present must contain ultimate savoring of the little things. Remember the study that reported that happier people savored the little things longer? Work toward this mindfulness of the present moment to truly appreciate happiness in its greatest, most alive sense.

How to Attain and Apply Happiness

But how does one attain complete happiness and apply it to one's life? Attempting to learn and co-habitat with self-love can be a true barrier; however, this barrier is the one thing preventing boosts in relationships, in careers, and in the rest of one's life. Nothing can get in the way.

1. Understand Yourself

Ask the question: what are my values and virtues? How do I talk to myself in my interior monologue? Are my words happy or negative? Identify yourself through your own eyes rather than reflecting upon what you think other people think of you.

2. BE HONEST AND OPEN WITH YOURSELF

You can't know if other people are lying to you; you can't know their truth. However, it is best to always be true to yourself. You can continue to tell yourself you're not good enough, or you can be honest: you can look to the strengths you know you have and tell yourself that you are good enough to uphold them in the greater society.

3. SLOW YOUR LIFE DOWN

Breathe. Life is going in all directions incredibly fast. Take a step back and check everything out. Ask yourself, mid-stress, what the worst thing that will happen is if you don't get everything done on time? Try to focus, instead, on the process at hand rather than the destination. Take your time, actively appreciate what you're doing, and you'll find happiness rushing toward you.

4. SEARCH FOR MEDITATION TIME

In this staggering, rushed society, the body and the brain has a disconnect. Your brain is constantly whirring, thinking about everything you must finish. However, a calm meditation can realign your body and your mind. Your mind can sense all the things you need on a biological level: are you hungry? Are you thirsty? It's important to reconnect with your body in order to activate true happiness.

5. FEEL LIMITLESS GRATITUDE

As aforementioned in the research chapter, those who feel gratitude reported feeling greater life happiness. If you look to your greater institution: the community in which you live, you can focus on gratitude for the relationships and virtues you have. Gratitude links you to other people, to relationships: therefore, focusing on it will remind you of the joy you feel when you have deep comradeship with another.

6. ACCEPT YOUR PRESENT FEELINGS

Remember that true happiness is often grayed with a fine line of unhappiness, providing the full range of human emotion. We are not humans without allowing everything in our own lives to affect us on a very personal, present level. In order to find true happiness, you must accept these feelings. Understanding a deep disappointment and feeling it allows you to push toward rectifying it and achieving later happiness.

7. HELP OTHERS

Remember what Seligman says. If your life is full of meaning and purpose, you will have true happiness. Your meaning and purpose could be rooted in assisting someone else. Research shows that helping those in need gives us real, internal value. Doing acts of kindness further shows your gratitude for the life you already have, thus allowing the relationship link to formulate.

8. FORGIVE YOURSELF FOR PAST AFFLICTIONS

Seligman also said that you must stop beating yourself up about past events. In order to feel happiness, you must make peace with yourself. Try to find the ways in which you learned from the past ordeals and apply them to the present and the future. Allow this growth to charge your optimism for the future.

9. USE YOUR DUCHENNE SMILE

Remember the baseball players from the 1952 playing cards? Those who were smiling in their photos lived up to eight years longer than the players who weren't smiling. If their lives weren't filled with joy—as demonstrated in their smiles—they wouldn't have had the strength or the care to live as long as they did. Smile a little longer; use all those muscles. A smile is contagious as well, passing along positive psychology and satisfaction to the masses. A happy community is a better community.

10. LOOK AT YOUR ENVIRONMENT

Think of the environmental positive psychology study in which residents of intellectual San Francisco reported less quality of happiness than those in Omaha, Nebraska—where love, not intellectualism is held above all. If you are lonely or lack human relationships, you might want to head to a community that has a better balance of both head happiness and heart happiness.

HAPPINESS BENEFITS

The benefits of happiness are broad. Think of the happiness factor in the lives of the baseball players outlined in the first happiness research project. The men who exhibited signs of true happiness lived a great deal longer. Therefore, if one attains happiness, one has a better quality of life—a life one wishes to hold onto for a bit longer.

Furthermore, happiness leads to greater physical activity. When one is happy, one wants to be on the move, to see things. One engages in exercise and team sports. One has higher self-esteem and therefore feels the confidence to work toward these outdoor joys. And this happiness leads to greater happiness, as well. Exercise lends endless endorphins which beat back against stress and depression.

Happiness allows fresh perspective on learning, as well. For example, when teachers make the classroom a happy, engaging place, students often pick up on the material a lot better. Therefore, any speaker or educator should hold both entertainment and knowledge at the forefront of the platform.

Sadness and anger—happiness' ugly cousins—actually cause several health defects like high blood pressure and stroke. Dr. Barbara Fredrickson conducted a study in which several stressed patrons watched a happy, funny movie. Afterwards, these patrons had a quicker heart rate recovery. Therefore, Fredrickson's theory maintains that happiness undoes stress effects, lending a happier, healthier life.

Chapter 5. Learned Optimism and Hope versus Helplessness

Understand how to achieve optimism and hope and ultimately refute helplessness and pessimism.

The Difference Between Optimism and Helplessness

The positive psychology idea of learned optimism allows an optimistic outlook on future situations. It is, therefore, a prime component of true happiness and positivity. As Seligman outlines, optimism for the future is intrinsic in promoting happiness. In order to create learned optimism, one must fight back against negative thoughts. These negative thoughts take the form of helplessness in the face of the future; one's helplessness forces one not to take charge of one's future, thus allowing one's self to fail or not work for future happiness.

Seligman maintains that one must change one's thoughts in order to back away from complete helplessness and reach toward optimism. There are three categories of basic differences from eternal helplessness and pessimism and learned optimism:

1. The Issue of Permanence

Learned optimists understand that bad events are not permanent. They do not allow bad events to follow them throughout the rest of their lives, stalking them and affecting future events. Furthermore, they believe that

27

good events occur for permanent, life-affirming reasons; good events will stick around and affect future outcomes. The incredible difference between optimists and pessimists lies in this line: optimists blame temporary, transient things for bad events; helpless, pessimistic people blame permanent things—things that will stick around and continue to cause raucous. And in this way, the pessimistic people actually allow negative reactions to remain in their lives.

2. THE ISSUE OF PERVASIVENESS

After feelings of helplessness or failure, optimistic people tend to block the feelings away and refuse to feel them anymore. They tend to group them away from future successes in order to not remind themselves of negativity. Helpless, pessimistic people, however, assume that one failure leads to another. They internalize the failure and understand that failure will follow them.

3. THE ISSUE OF PERSONALIZATION

Optimists look at bad events and blame outside sources; they do not naturally give themselves the blame, therefore allowing themselves to work toward greater goals. Pessimists, however, blame themselves for everything. Therefore, optimists go into situations with a great deal of confidence, looking for all that's available to them. Pessimists aren't ready to feel confidence when they're weighed down with blame.

HOW TO ACHIEVE OPTIMISM

Becoming an optimist means formulating new habits in order to incorporate a brighter, happier outlook.

1. ALTER THE WAYS YOU TELL YOUR STORIES

Tell your stories without placing the blame of what happened on yourself. Think of negative events as things that don't relate to future events. Remember that placing the negative blame on yourself beats back against confidence and therefore hinders your chances for future successes.

2. REMEMBER TO FORGIVE

The past is in the past; therefore, any past faults you've committed to yourself or to others must remain tucked away. Forgive your friends and family for anything they've done, as well; don't maintain the pessimism that people will hurt you in the future.

3. RECORD THE EVENTS OF THE DAY

An important, research driven tip is to think always in threes. Every evening, write three positive things for every negative thing you remember or write. This way, you can counteract the pessimism in your brain and look with optimism toward the next day.

BENEFITS OF OPTIMISM

Fueled with the realization that they don't have to hold onto past traumas, optimists tend to push beyond all boundaries. They do better in school, succeed in their hobbies, and have fulfilling work experiences.

Pessimists, on the other hand, give up easily. They feel the weight of depression and complete helplessness in the face of the future.

CHAPTER 6. MINDFULNESS: POSITIVE PSYCHOLOGY AND BALANCE

Achieve balance and work through stress with the positive psychology conception: mindfulness.

WHAT IS MINDFULNESS?

Mindfulness is an awareness of interior body sensations, feelings, conscious thoughts, and the environment. One feels the awareness without added judgment; one focuses on every moment that passes, living in the very present, at the very forefront of existence. It allows one to find true peace in the midst of uncertainty; it further activates one from making automatic decisions, allowing one to concentrate on the ways in which one's actions will affect one's greater life. It allows one to join many sections of one's thoughts together as a whole.

Therefore, one can achieve greater positivity through mindfulness. One can focus on the past and the reasons why the past events do not have to affect one's future. One can eliminate feelings of pessimism because they will affect one's confidence. One can feel completely whole and concentrated in the greater joys and fulfillments of life.

HOW TO ACHIEVE MINDFULNESS

Achieving mindfulness in the middle of the day can de-activate stress and allow better formation of future events. Reach toward mindfulness for true health and confidence.

1. CHOOSE A SOLITARY, IDEAL LOCATION IN ORDER TO MEDITATE

This place should be wholly unobtrusive. It should not be too hot or too cold; it should not be too dark or too light. It should be a plan in which you feel safe.

2. POSITION YOURSELF IN AN APPROPRIATE POSTURE

The posture you choose is up to you. Standing, sitting, lying down, or walking can all allow positive meditation depending on the ways in which you'd like to proceed. Walking is perhaps the most simplistic. You can find mindfulness as you walk along, incorporating it in your everyday life. You can focus on various parts of your body: how your feet move, how your knees bend, or how your toes fold on top of the pavement. All of these things are things that are happening in the moment, and therefore must be incorporated in proper mindfulness.

3. FOCUS ON ONE TASK AT A TIME

Do not multitask. Multitasking forces you to become scattered; you are far more productive when your mind is wholly focused on the task at hand.

4. TRY ELIMINATING THINGS FROM YOUR TO-DO LIST

How much do you have to do in order to be happy? How many hobbies, how many sports do you have to be involved in? If you choose just a few things to really work toward, you can fuel your concentration and become inherently mindful, less scattered.

5. EAT SLOWLY

Savor your food. Remember the study that found that people who were happier savored their chocolate bar for longer than the people who felt harried and unhappy? Remember that you eat your food to fuel yourself, of course, but that it should also taste good and formulate a pleasure.

6. MEDITATE WHILE YOU COOK AND CLEAN

Clean and cook slowly, noticing your every movement and the slow way in which things form before you: the slow way the stovetop becomes clean or the way the vegetables brown in the pan. Notice the little things and appreciate the process in order to create deep mindfulness for yourself.

BENEFITS OF MINDFULNESS

Being mindful allows complete appreciation for the present moment. It allows one to knock off the stresses of the future or the unhappy events of the past in order to exist ever-so-simply in the world. One can find the benefits of mindfulness in improved sleep levels, in the alleviation of stomach difficulties, and in the decrease of blood pressure.

Furthermore, mindfulness works to improve one's mental health. If one is suffering from depression, eating disorders, anxiety disorders, or obsessive-compulsive disorder, one can reach to mindfulness in order to compartmentalize one's life and see it more clearly, more precisely. Only with full, intrinsic mindfulness can one truly imbibe happiness.

Chapter 7. Flow: The Drive to Succeed

What is Flow?

Flow is an intricate study in positive psychology, one introduced by positive psychologist Mihaly Csikszentmihalyi. Hear the word "flow." What does one think of? Perhaps one thinks of a river: how one thing flows easily and rapidly into the next thing. Every part precedes a different part; every part is aligned. But how does this relate to the body and the brain? How does this relate to positive psychology and the steps to further one's self to greater life satisfaction?

Essentially, in relation to body and mind, flow is the complete focus and attention to a single activity. One is devoted to it; one can see nothing else except the commitment in that single moment. Imagine the very end of a race in which one pushes the limits of the body; in which one allows all muscles, all tendons, and all brain waves to anticipate and work toward the big finish. The brain lends no energy to think about the grocery list or dropping the kids off at soccer practice. Time rushes away, and the brain makes no notice. One's ego is completely removed; one no longer maintains a sense of self. Each movement follows a sequence of events geared toward this series of flow maintenance: like a river following the same path, one's movements gear like a single unit toward a common goal.

The Flow Experience: 10 Factors

Positive psychologist Mihaly Csikszentmihalyi outlines the ten factors involved in the flow experience.

1. Challenging yet practical, attainable goals.
2. Complete focus.
3. The activity that renders the experience of flow is rewarding on a mental level.
4. One loses all concept of self-consciousness. One feels at-home in one's skin.
5. One loses track of time; the goal abstracts the presence of regular time.
6. Ready, available feedback achieved after reaching the goal.
7. One has an understanding that the goal is doable with regards to one's skill levels.
8. One maintains a feeling of control over the outcome of the reach.
9. One no longer thinks of physical, biological needs.
10. The focus lives wholly in the activity.

EXAMPLES OF FLOW

Flow can happen in every aspect in one's life: one can become wholly enthralled, for example, in attaining a fully clean kitchen and will thus clean the burners, the back of the stove, beneath the chairs without realizing that one's elbow and knees are aching. Flow is incredibly useful, however, when applied to three spectrums of one's life.

1. EDUCATION AND FLOW

Flow experiences have been researched with regards to education. Csikszentmihalyi suggested that when one overlearns or over-works for a concept, one might achieve a renewed sense of flow. Essentially, the over-learned information is a part of one's thought process; it has been played over and over in one's mind, therefore becoming a semblance of one's thoughts. This relates back to the first, primary theories of flow: one's complete focus weighs heavily on this one activity. One lives wholly in the activity of learning and broadening one's mind.

Furthermore, positive psychologist researcher Csikszentmihalyi offered that when one stretches one's abilities in order to attempt to learn something else, one may experience the drive of flow. Essentially, this concept keeps goals constantly out of arm's reach, allowing one to consistently remain in that period of flow—of constant learning.

2. SPORTS AND FLOW

Understanding the way in which flow applies to sports settings requires just a bit of imagination. The reach toward sport achievement is designed much the way the reach toward educational achievement is. However, the sport flow breaks its way from the mind to the muscles and the heart and the bones. One's brain sends constant signals to allow these body sectors to keep working toward the goal. Just like the educational flow, the sport goal is just out of reach. However, one understands one's ability to achieve this goal. One loses one's sense of self and carries ultimate mastery in physical performance.

3. WORK ENVIRONMENT AND FLOW

Flow can activate the mind in any dull workplace environment. If one is stimulated by personal goals—just out of reach and challenging to attain—one can receive this over-arching feeling of flow. If one is churning out a novel, for example, one might put all one's attention toward the task at hand, forgetting completely about any other errands or relationship activity. Because finishing this novel will allow one to reach full self-achievement— for now, until one reaches for more goals and more flow—it is incredibly beneficial in the field of positive psychology. Prospering in work environments prescribes to both the self-esteem and the self-actualization stages on the Maslow Hierarchy of Needs. Flow provides a steady grasp of these sectors.

How to Attain and Apply Flow

Reaching the flow state allows assurance and happiness; it pushes one's boundaries, allowing tasks to reach beyond their initial states to things greater and unforeseen. Flow can apply to everyday things, as well: things one does around the house, exercise, and work production. Work through the five steps to achieve flow and see if flow leads to a greater path of self-actualization.

1. Match the Skill Level to the Task at Hand

Flow occurs when one's skill aligns itself to a goal. As aforementioned, in order to achieve flow, one must feel that the goal is do-able, if challenging. For example: if one studies incredibly for a test, one might achieve a sense of flow while achieving the goal: taking the test. If one has trained for a marathon, one might feel that sense of flow while completing the task one has so well prepared for.

2. Work for a Challenge

One can achieve a sense of flow if one pushes and stretches one's abilities just the smallest bit. Therefore, one's skills already match that which is desired to achieve; however, these skills are stretched. For example: an artist decides to move from watercolors to acrylics in order to achieve a sense of flow. This artist already has mastery over the paintbrush; however, this artist will work to achieve mastery over the acrylic medium.

3. Attach Real, Legitimate Goals to Your Cause

Flow occurs when strategic goals formulate in one's mind. One's purpose for committing to the task should be complete and without argument.

4. Do Not Multitask or Seek Interruption

All of one's concentration must be devoted to only the task. Multitasking forces the brain into semi-concentration of several different things, therefore disallowing the feeling of flow.

5. Focus on the Process

It is easy for one to rely heavily on the idea of the end of the goal. After one achieves this end goal, one can finally take a rest. One can focus on other things. However, if one is inherently focused on the end result, one will not experience flow. One must focus upon one's process in arriving to the end state. After all, flow is the journey; the goal is the destination.

FLOW BENEFITS AFTER APPLICATION

Attaining flow offers several benefits that push for greater, more satisfactory lives: lives fueled with self-actualization and attainment of goals.

Research has proven that flow actually enhances performance. If one regularly dips into the flow experience when one is doing something, one has the movement, the power down an a very physical and mental level. Flow can enhance one's performance in a broad smattering of areas such as creativity, athletics, learning, and teaching.

Furthermore, flow can actually push one to attain greater learning and development. After one achieves one's goal after the feeling of flow encapsulates, one receives a sense of full mastery; one has conquered the experience and received the benefits of the goal. However, this essentially means that one's interests are no longer captured by this goal: something attained is no longer a goal, right? Therefore, one must work toward a new goal, honing one's skills and working toward a new mastery: one that allows a push toward this goal and a new, thriving sense of flow.

This constant application of flow will help one to attain effortless self-actualization and achieve a greater sense of self.

CHAPTER 8. CHARACTER STRENGTHS AND VIRTUES

Positive psychologists Christopher Peterson and Martin Seligman wrote a book called The Character Strengths and Virtues in order to bring a theoretical framework to positive psychology. They outline twenty-four character strengths in human beings. In their book, human character strengths satisfy the following criteria:

1. They must be fulfilling.
2. They must be intrinsically valuable in that they cannot be squandered like material possessions.
3. They hold no rivalry.
4. They are habitual; therefore, they are a part of one's traits.
5. These strengths are personified by popular people. For example, Martin Luther King Jr. personifies hope.
6. Societal norms and institutions attempt to nurture these strengths.

When one practices these character strengths and virtues, one is contributing to humanity and also to one's interior happiness. These character strengths stem from five basic categories of strengths and virtues.

1. KNOWLEDGE

Knowledge and wisdom-based character strengths include creativity, curiosity, love of learning, and open-mindedness.

2. BRAVERY AND COURAGE

These strengths include persistence, integrity, vitality, love, kindness, and humanity.

3. JUSTICE

These strengths include fairness, leadership, and a sense of social responsibility and loyalty.

4. TEMPERANCE AND LACK OF EXCESS

These strengths include forgiveness, prudence, self-regulation, and forgiveness.

5. TRANSCENDENCE AND SEARCH FOR MEANING

These strengths include gratitude, hope, spirituality, humor, and appreciation of beauty.

APPLY CHARACTER STRENGTHS AND VIRTUES

One's character strengths and virtues align like traits in one's personality. Understand the goals you have and whether or not your personal character strengths fit into this fold. For example, if you have great creativity, you can align your creativity to forge ahead in a creative goal environment. If you assign your life to your character strengths, you will reach a higher level of self-actualization; you are meant to be working with these skills. You will feel your at your best. Your strengths, after all, are different than other people's strengths.

Positive psychology maintains that developing and utilizing your strengths allows for increased flow, positive thinking, and greater happiness. Understand what you're good at and what you feel fulfilled in. Research shows that if you activate these strengths in all areas of your life, your chances of depression will decrease significantly.

Chapter 9. Positive Thinking: A Process

What is Positive Thinking?

Positive thinking in the field of positive psychology relates to the ways in which one looks at life. How does one perceive it? Is this perception positive or negative? Positive psychology understands positive thinking and its roll in instilling happiness and fulfillment.

Positive thinking does not mean one looks at the world simplistically, without an understanding of the dangers and challenges associating with living that life. No. Positive thinking means that one approaches all of life: the challenges and the joys, with a positive mindset. With positive thinking, one can make the most out of any situation. One looks at abilities positively, viewing them as strengths that will push one forward to fulfillment. One is able to see one's self in the greater picture as a content and cooperative, vibrant part of one's society.

Positive Thinking and Explanatory Style

Martin Seligman, positive psychologist researcher, has analyzed something called "explanatory style" in order to understand whether or not someone has positive or negative thinking. Explanatory style relates to how someone pegs "blame" or "credit" when explaining a story after the fact.

Essentially, if one explains a story from one's life in a positive manner, one gives credit to one's self for what has happened—if, of course, it is due. Positive thinkers blame negative outcomes on exterior sources, as well, displacing the blame from themselves with the understanding that blame would just slow them down. They understand, as positive thinkers, that negative thinking and negative events are just fleeting. Nothing terrible holds permanence.

Conversely, negative thinking with regards to explanatory style forces blame onto one's self. One does not congratulate or feel the invested rewards after achieving a goal. Instead, one reflects all negativity back on one's self and remains in a hole of self-doubt and uncertainty.

HOW TO ATTAIN AND APPLY POSITIVE THINKING

In order to attain positive thinking and incorporate it into daily life, one must understand one's currents thoughts and how these affect one's life. Pay attention to the inner-dialogue, the inner-voice in order to understand the interior brain images and descriptions. Is there a negative consciousness attacking one's brain, working against one's self-fulfillment? Is there serious mental criticism?

Ridding one's self of these negative thoughts is incredibly difficult. It's best to start small. Identify one area of life that is most affected by negativity. This area could be, for example, one's appearance. Due to constant comparing to other people, one can find unrest about one's appearance. However, one can allow this realization—that negative thoughts are fueling the unhappiness with one's looks—to actually beat back against all negative thinking and formulate positive thinking. Pegging a specific area of one's life in order to rectify the situation makes the situation a bit easier to manage.

Once one has chosen one's specific, negativity-boosting area in one's life, one must focus on those thoughts. When one feels the negativity sweeping through one's body, one must stop and think. One must understand the ways in which any negativity can become a positivity. One cannot allow this unfortunate uncertainty to become an affecting part of one's life. Alter these thoughts as much as possible; one must remind one's self that one is worthy for things and for speaking well of one's self. Words become a fire beneath the topic: words can either stifle it and die by being hard and strict and negative; otherwise, they can fuel one to better self-fulfillment and brighter future days.

In order to positively affect one's interior life, one must allow positivity to swoop through one's mind and alter the way in which one perceives the entirety of one's life. One must choose to become a better dialogue to one's self.

POSITIVE THINKING BENEFITS

Positive Thinking provides many over-arching life benefits. Those consistent comments from peers urging to "look on the bright side of life" actually maintain a good, researched perspective.

For example, those who actively work with positive thinking can activate better stress-coping strategies. When positive thinkers, optimists, encounter a situation that creates stress in them, they decide to ask for assistance or work toward the goal in a different, more energetic way. They change something about themselves in a positive light in order to activate another road. Non-positive thinkers, the pessimists, instead view all negative situations as things they cannot control; they feel that it is useful for them to push forward and persevere. Therefore, positive thinking provides plenty of forward-motion and rejuvenation.

Chapter 10. Resilience and the Strength to Move Forward

What Is Resilience?

Resilience is the calm in the face of a great storm. It is the ultimate, positive answer to inevitable setbacks in one's life: setbacks relating to relationships, the workplace, or the environment. People that utilize resilience are able to cope with these setbacks incredibly; they do not become overwhelmed but rather utilize their characteristic virtues and strengths in order to realize a victory over the situation.

It is important to note that the surge of resilience does not completely eliminate basic human feelings like stress. Resilience, rather, allows one the strength necessary to tackle difficulties in the best, most level-headed manner possible. Resilience is often a learned trait, one that can assist a whole range of people in their future problems.

How to Achieve Resilience

One can build a resilience in order to attack future life events without feeling the constant defeat from stress and feelings.

1. Believe in Yourself

Understand your strengths and virtuous characteristics. These characteristics will assist you in future setbacks; remember them and reach for them when you need them. You have all the capabilities to work through any life problem.

2. DEVELOP RELATIONSHIPS AND BUILD A NETWORK

You do not have to do anything alone. Work to build close human relationships with people around you; they'll look to you in times of crisis just as you can look to them during times of crisis in your life. You can share your negative feelings with them while working positively toward an ultimate outcome.

3. MAINTAIN OPTIMISM

Hoping hope for the future is incredibly important in order to understand that whatever you're currently trying to overcome will ultimately result in something great. It will not affect future events, and it is not your fault. Setbacks will come and go; optimism is here to stay.

4. UNDERSTAND YOUR GOALS

When a situation begins to overwhelm you, take a deep breath and step back. Make a goal list for what you want to happen with regards to the situation, and break down the steps you must follow in order to achieve these goals. Compartmentalizing your goals through the storm will allow the storm to seem smaller, more manageable.

BENEFITS OF RESILIENCE

Maintaining emotional resilience allows one to beat back against both mental and physical negative reactions to events. One can reside in a truly happy, healthy environment with all the tools one requires in order to string that happiness past any possible setbacks.

Negative emotions due to setbacks and a lack of resilience lead to an increase of the stress hormone, cortisol, which ultimately leads to inflammation and increased illness. One can feel depressed and hopeless without the surge of resilience; one cannot see happiness as a viable option.

Resilience—along with sheer happiness, positive thinking, and mindfulness—all push toward a truly wonderful existence. This is an existence not without flaws, not without stressors. However, it is an existence one can truly thrive within. It is an existence in which one can recognize one's virtues and strengths. One can fulfill true satisfaction and self-actualization. One can find one's self.

ABOUT THE AUTHOR

The mission of Jonny Bell is to be able to help inspire and change the world, one reader at a time.

This author wants to provide the most amazing life tools that anyone can apply into their lives. It doesn't matter whether you have hit rock bottom in your life or your life is amazing and you want to keep taking it to another level.

If you are like this writer, then you are probably looking to become the best version of yourself. You are likely not to settle for an okay life. You want to live an extraordinary life. Not only to be filled within but also to contribute to society.

He has been studying and applying psychology for over 5 years and met a lot of interesting people along the way. With these writings, Bell wants to keep inspiring others to change for the better.

OTHER BOOKS BY JONNY BELL

SPORTS PSYCHOLOGY: INSIDE THE ATHLETE'S MIND

Have You Ever Wanted To Improve Your Performance? No matter what sport you play, there are always problems with confidence and motivation that can get in the way of actually using all of the skills that you have been working to build through your entire life. That is where sports psychology comes in.

With the help of this book, you will be able to: Build confidence that helps you become unstoppable. Visualize your way to success so that you know what to expect.

Set goals that will help you measure improvements and strive towards specific markers.

Learn how to help others to do the same. By combining simple techniques with a high quality understanding of psychology, you will have everything at your disposal to take your performance to the next level and find success that you never thought possible previously.

SOCIAL PSYCHOLOGY: A PRACTICAL GUIDE TO THE HUMAN MIND

Understanding why people do what they do is an essential skills to have. When you understand why the people around you do what they do, you are able to avoid a lot of drama and conflict.

51

Throughout history society has had a profound influence in people's actions

This book was written to fulfill a simple mission: to educate people from all walks of life about the importance and application of social psychology in their day-to-day lives.

This book was not written to make science intimidating, not to mention boring. The aim is to show how a serious and legitimate science like social psychology could be easily understood and appreciated by non-psychology majors, practically by every 'man on the street'.

Are you any of the following?
Simply curious about how human minds work, especially in a group or social setting, but won't bother digging complicated science stuff
Wants to have something productive to do during free time, regardless of what it is
A freshman/woman in a general psychology major
Undecided on what major to take in university/college

If any, this book is for you!

COGNITIVE BEHAVIORAL THERAPY: CBT ESSENTIALS AND FUNDAMENTALS

There's no reason to live a life without fulfillment or excitement. In our modern world, we see people struggling with depression, anxiety, anger, etc. Psychologist and counselors have been using Cognitive Behavioral Therapy to solve all these struggles.
A Practical Guide to CBT and Modern Psychology will allow anyone to use CBT in their lives.

Positive Psychology

It doesn't matter whether or not you have a background in Psychology. In this comprehensive guide you will learn all the fundamentals used in CBT by therapists.

Inside you will be exposed to the following:

CBT History
Techniques
When and How to use CBT
Examples
Methods to help others with psychological struggles

And much more

If you're ready to understand and use the powerful techniques of Cognitive Behavioral Therapy, then this is an excellent guide.

EMOTIONAL INTELLIGENCE: A PRACTICAL GUIDE TO MASTERING EMOTIONS: EMOTIONS HANDBOOK AND JOURNAL

Understanding emotions is one of the most important aspects of personal development and growth

Without truly mastering our emotions we run a high risk in behaving without awareness.

Throughout years society has come to believe that our level of IQ will determine the success of a person's life. However, in recent years psychologist have found new insight by studying successful people. The results have been surprising because what determines a person's life success is not IQ but rather EI.

53

Emotional Intelligence (EI) is the foundation of living a successful and meaningful life. People who succeed in life have a tremendous awareness of their emotions.

Inside this book, you will be on the path of living a life that includes the following

Emotional Mastery

Awareness of your own emotions and others

Effortlessly redirecting your emotions

A deeper connection with the people you love

Do not allow your emotions to take over your life and instead master the art of your emotions today!

ONE LAST THING...

If you enjoyed this book or found it useful I'd be very grateful if you'd post a short review on Amazon. Your support really does make a difference and I read all the reviews personally so I can get your feedback and make this book even better.

Thanks again for your support!

Made in the USA
San Bernardino, CA
12 July 2019